AF418420

In the Deluge

poetry that flows

In the Deluge

Dana Lockhart

ISBN-13: 979-8-9856538-1-6

Published by Grigori Press LLC.,
P.O. Box 137, New London, MO 63459.
www.grigoripress.com

www.danalockhart.com

*This book of poetry
is dedicated to anyone
who has ever made me laugh, smile, scream, or cry.
If you are one of those people,
then there might be a poem in here about you.*

Sorry about that.

Foreword

Chance encounters have the power to forge deep connections, and luck often leads us to remarkable individuals. Such was the case when I had the pleasure of meeting Dana Lockhart at a 2019 book signing event, where we were both signing authors. Little did I know that our paths would intersect again through the pages of "In the Deluge."

As a poet humbled by the recognition of three Goodreads Choice Award nominations, I am privileged to be entrusted with the honor of writing this foreword.

Stepping into this poetry collection was to wade deep into the uncertainty of life, the drowning of unrequited love, and the familiar ache of the darkness of the human spirit. I recognized a likeness in how empaths often drown in our hearts and minds, uncertain and triumphant in our desire to put pen to paper, to immortalize our hurt. I languished in the vivid imagery and the clever rhymes, losing myself to the power of poetry and how it weaves tales.

"In the Deluge" is a testament to Dana Lockhart's artistry. She skillfully paints a poignant picture with each line, inviting readers to embark on an introspective voyage of self-discovery, longing, the murky path of love unreturned, and a longing for a life outside the writer's mind we often find ourselves trapped in—only able to reveal our hearts in darkness and ink, never aloud. Through verse, she offers solace, understanding, and a profound connection to those who have felt the weight of their emotions.

Within these pages, you will discover the depths of the human spirit, verses that touch the very core of our being. Lockhart's poetic voice envelops us with each turn of the page, creating an atmosphere that mirrors the ebb and flow of life's unpredictable tides. Her words become a life force, propelling us into realms where emotions run deep and serve as a sanctuary for those who seek solace in the written word. It is an oasis—offering respite and understanding.

Lockhart's keen ability to evoke vivid imagery reminds me of the power of poetry to bridge the gap between our innermost thoughts and the world around us. We access the depths of her own experiences through Lockhart's words, yet we also find ourselves reflected in the universal truths she unveils. Through this shared connection, we discover the true essence of humanity and the transformative nature of art.

"In the Deluge" invites us to embrace our vulnerability and navigate the storms that rage within. It is a testament to the resilience of the human spirit and the capacity for growth and renewal. Dana Lockhart's words hold the power to uplift, inspire, and heal, providing a guiding light in the darkest of times.

-J.R. Rogue

jrrogue.com

Sea of Sorrows

THE SHAPE OF A SOUL I.

If I am wrong,
And there is such a thing as a soul,
I imagine them to be like snowflakes,
Every one distinct and unique,
Different colors, shades, and shapes.
Some made out of autumn leaves
And others made from dew drops.
Some burning hot and loud,
And others cold and quiet.

And when I picture my soul,
I imagine rain clouds,
Gray and stormy.
The storm is not violent,
With lightning or thunder,
Nor is it a heavy downpour
With hurricane winds.
But the rain, it never ends,
And the sun, it rarely shines.
A perpetual rainstorm,
Gentle and quiet, steady and slow,
Always on the verge of flooding,
But not quite drowning anything.

My heart is heavy with all the water.

And maybe that is why
I love a rainy day,
Because the gray,
And the clouds,
And the rain,
Are just like me.

LIMERENCE

Can I be sad for a while?
Please don't ask me what is wrong.
Leave me to my wallowing
And let me drown in my tears.
Really, it is good for me
To let all the feelings out.
I would rather they be free
Than fester inside my heart.
So, bring on the thunderstorm!
And let me ride out the rain.
I'll be better come the morn
If I just weather the pain.

LET IT GO

Still holding onto you is like
Trying to caress an old flame
When I know from experience
Playing with the fire will burn.

Trying to keep ahold of you
Is like grasping at the sheer face
Of the side of a mountain range.
The fall is inevitable.

Like sand slipping through my fingers
And catching water in a sieve,
Like trying to capture lightning
Or trying to forget breathing.

Trying to cling to what remains
Seems better than just letting go,
Because if we can just move on—
You, and me, and the memories—
Did it even matter at all?

Against a Feather

My heart is feeling heavy;
For what reason today?
Is it full to the brim with salt water,
Or frozen solid into ice?
Or, perhaps, it turned to stone.
It's hard to tell sometimes;
It just does this on its own.

FRIEND

Sadness
Is my truest friend,
For its always there for me
When things come to an end.
When I need help,
And when I cry,
When I'm alone,
And when I sigh.
I can always count on sadness,
To catch me when I fall.
It's what good friends do,
After all.

Hey, Stranger

I know it's been a while,
And we both have things to do,
But wouldn't it be nice
For old time's sake,
To let go and act as though
Time had been kinder to us,
And the distance not so wide,
That all the time we spent growing
Had not grown us apart.
Can we just play pretend
It's a late night on a weekend
Some ten years ago or so,
When it was just you, and me,
And not a care in the world.

SHOWER

Today I took a shower
To wash you away.
I scrubbed off your touch,
Washed away the tears,
And blasted away your heat
With the cold, cleansing spray.
And when it was over,
All that was left was me.
Naked, cold, and alone.

But cleaning my body
Did not clean my soul,
And tear stains anew
Ran streaks down my face.
It was the best I could do.

Brunette

I have wanted to ask you why
Perhaps a hundred times
Why you never loved me.

Was it something that I said,
Or the way that I dressed,
Or are you just not into brunettes?

Cast Away

You should have warned me
That you were the type who
Threw away your broken things
Like they meant nothing to you
Instead of trying to fix them
Before you chose to break me.

REGRET

I have no regrets,
And I swear this is true.
Yes, there are things,
I wish I could undo,
Some people I once knew
I wish I had never met,
But this does not alone
Become something I regret.
For if I took any of it back,
I'd lose far more than I'd gain.
Who I have and who I am
Was worth all of the pain.

MENDING

Everything is temporary,
And that is a comfort,
For this, too, shall pass,
As did all things before.
Time mends all broken things
And erodes that which remains.

AGAIN AND AGAIN

Go ahead and break my heart.
It's not like it's unexpected.
I could see it coming miles away,
Yet I cared about you anyway.
You're not the first,
And won't be the last,
There is more heartache
Waiting in the future
And plenty more of it
Haunting in the past.
So hit me with it hard
Or break it to me gently,
It doesn't make a difference;
It will hurt the same way.

Undead

My mind wanders once again,
About what could have been.
But you were never interested.

Can a dream die if it never lived?

Desert

It's another lonely night
Without you by my side,
And even though I tried,
I can't get you off my mind.
But this is nothing new.

If each night was a grain of sand
And I had one for each evening
That you were here beside me
I could count them on one hand.

And if I had a grain of sand
For every night I was alone,
Yearning to hold you tight,
I would be lost in a desert.

PASSERSBY

You came into my life
As if you had always been there
And you left me behind
Like you were never here at all.

BLUE

Blue was never so beautiful
As I saw in your eyes that day,
And for the first time in my life,
I believed in a destiny;

That you and I were placed right here
In this moment for a purpose
And everything led up to this.
The world moved for me on that day.

For you, it was just Saturday.

SMOKE IN THE WIND

I did not cry
When I heard you died,
And still not a tear has fallen
I went back to bed,
Not a thought in my head;
I wonder if my heart is rotten.

Tear Stains

The only difference
Between tear stains
And blood drops
Is the color of the pain.

FIRST TIME

I cried the first time
I told you I loved you
And I didn't know why.

But you would be my biggest regret—
I just didn't know it yet.

THUNDER

The sound of thunder is never far away,
Rumbling like distant beating drums.
I am still waiting for the rain.

FOOL

It's the tempting trickster,
With a tongue of silver
Who steals the golden hearts
And collects them in jars,
But no amount of jest
Will fill its empty chest.

WAR

When the last two rivers ran red,
Not one among those left standing
Could tell which of the rivers flowed
With the blood of their enemies
Or the blood of their faithful friends.

Oceans of Wrath

SHAPE OF A SOUL III.

If my soul is a rain cloud,
Yours is the eye of the storm.
Empty, silent, and calm,
And surrounded by a hurricane.

It seemed to complement my own,
Both our souls were storms,
And where mine was mild,
Yours contained extremes.

I thought perhaps if I could fill
The void that was your eye,
That both our storms might clear,
But if that did not come to pass,
If we were destined to be storms,
At least we could weather it together.

But you weren't looking for rain,
You were looking for lightning,
As I was once looking for sun.
Something bold, something flashy,
Who struck you like a lightning rod.
And in my soul of perpetual rain,
No matter how hard I tried,
There was no place that was dry
For me to ignite that spark
That would turn me into a thunderstorm.

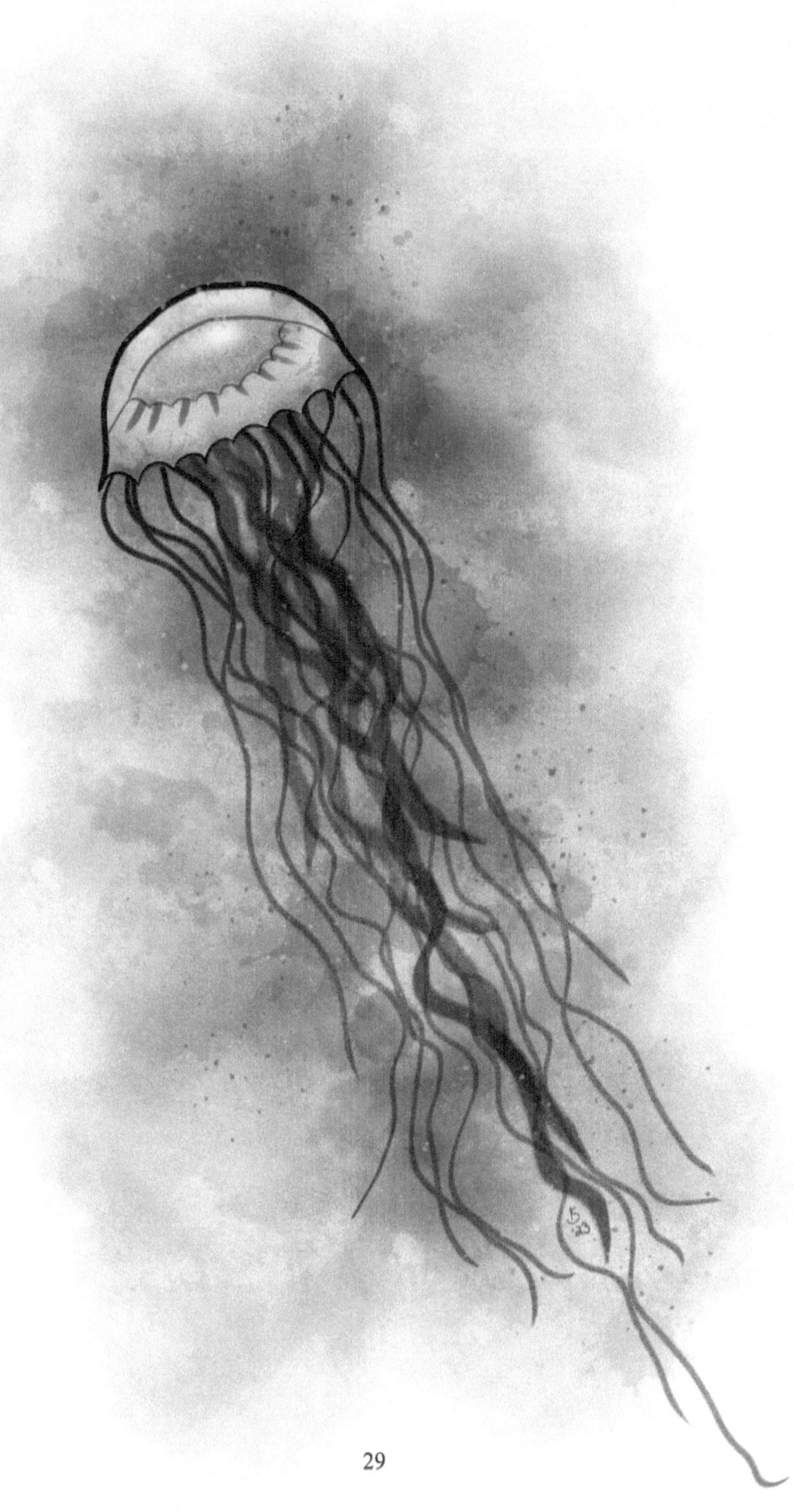

FALSE PROPHET

You caught my attention
With the way that you spoke.
Not with a silver tongue,
But with the care of an artist,
Considering every brushstroke.
In a world always screaming
Without reason or grace,
I found your words refreshing,
Both beautiful and unique.

For a while, I gave you my ear,
But when you did not return the gesture,
So too did I stop seeking to hear.
The facade began to crumble.
Your beautiful words lost meaning
And began to sound like everyone else's:
Just more noise in a chaotic world.

KARMA

I hope it hurt you
To hurt me
At least a little,
Because if it didn't,
Then it meant nothing.
Nothing at all.

PRAYER

I'm not saying I'm a believer
But this I know for sure:
I've done nothing to deserve
The hardships I endure.

So whoever may be listening,
Be it god, devil, or mortal man
Or forgotten eldritch horror
With any sense of justice
To right wrongs in the world,

Hear my prayer, and grant me
A much needed reprieve
From many a misfortune
And missed opportunity.

DRIVE

You can only drive me crazy
If I give you the keys,
And, boy, did I let you drive.
Through roller coaster hills
And winding back roads,
Shooting out over the clouds
Only to come crashing back down.

Some days the drive is sweet,
A beautiful day and a gentle breeze.
Let the top down, enjoy the view,
Like we have all the time in the world
To just go wherever we want to.

On other days the road is rough
And you drive us straight off a cliff
And we hit every rock and tree
On the way down, crashing, burning,
The whiplash alone tears me apart.
The crash leaves scars, deep and raw,
Making me wonder, was the ride worth it all?

So I try and take away the keys
Because, again, I've had enough,
Enough of your reckless driving,
Enough of being a passenger of my own life,
But your eyes, they beg me for one more ride.
Don't go, they say, don't leave me alone.

And it's a beautiful day, the sun is shining,
The highway is full of opportunity.
Maybe this ride will be different,
And we'll go down a road we hadn't gone on,
I hope, so we go for another spin
And I let you drive me crazy once again.

A Real Poem

Well-placed words and fanciful phrases
Are what a poem makes.
However, there are days
When just the right word
Does not contain elegance or grace.
Sometimes, the only word to express
The tumultuous feelings inside
Is to scream—*fuck!*—at the top of your lungs
And call it goddamn poetry.

ONE OF THESE THINGS

Wild wind whispers in the wood;
Not much more makes movement.
Here and there critters creep
On pitter-pattering paws.
The colorful, cool collage
Of leaves and lilacs leave
Sweet scents in the spring.
Lingering light leaks
Between barked branches
Onto moist, murky mud,
Reflecting on rubbish—
Coca Cola™ can.

This poem was awarded 2nd place in the St. Louis Writers Guild Dean Wagner Poetry Contest in 2018.

WORDLESS

The most elegant poem
Cannot contain my tears.
The most beautiful words
Cannot describe the pain.
Simple beats and meter
Cannot make sense of it.

Hiding my feelings within rhymes;
It's all just a waste of time.

If I can't understand it,
Then neither will you.

UNLIKE ME

There was a time
I thought you just like me,
One of the cursed ones,
Burdened with knowledge
But wiser for it.
I thought, for the first time,
That I was no longer alone.

But as it turned out
You were not different at all.
And were, in fact,
Just like everyone else.
A fool, a disaster,
And nothing like me at all.

I contain oceans
And you are a raindrop.

Mother Earth

If you believe the Earth cannot feel,
Listen to the pouring rain;
Feel the tears drowning the world.
Listen again to the thunder;
Feel the anger bristling in the storm.
Listen to the hurricane;
Feel the dying screams of the Earth.
If you believe the Earth cannot speak,
Then you have not been listening.

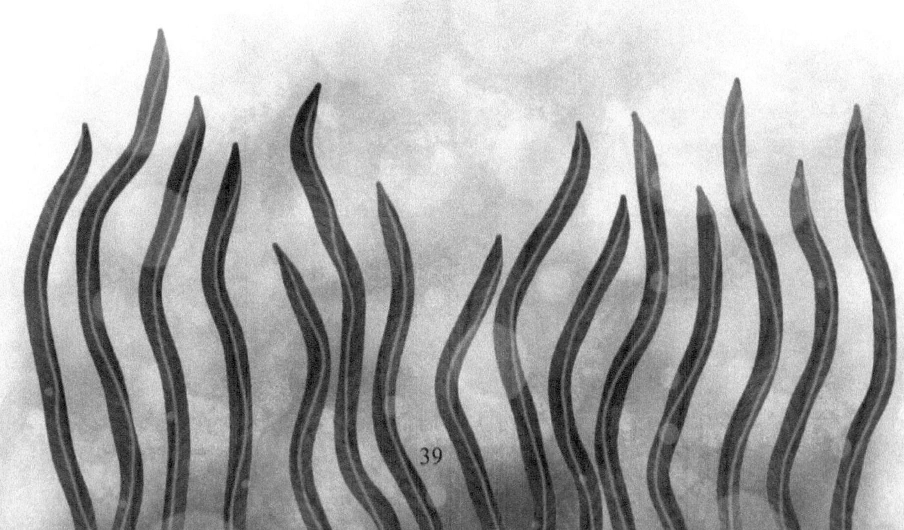

MASOCHIST

It's not as though I enjoy the pain,
So don't call me a masochist.
But never was there a better teacher
Than broken dreams and promises.
After all, pain is only temporary,
But the lessons learned are infinite.

Never After

When I saw you
I saw a future
Like I had always dreamed.

When you saw me
You saw a friend
And that would never change.

NAMELESS

The worst fate I can imagine,
Is not painful or terrifying,
But quite the opposing feeling.
Imagine, for a moment,
That your life had no meaning,
And left no impact at all.
Imagine, if you can,
That when you leave this world
Not a soul will remember your name.
This is a fate most terrible,
Perfect for someone like ██████.

WRITE IT DOWN

Maybe I am a writer
Because it's easier to say
What I am thinking when no one is watching.

Maybe I write poetry
Because of all the years
I spent in silence because no one was listening.

The Fall of an Empire

I promise I'm not angry,
I feel more akin to Achilles
When his eyes fell upon Patroclus
Lying still at Hector's feet.

River of Dreams

ANGELS & DEMONS

I have known angels
With razor-blade wings
Who told gilded lies
And demons who saved lives
While wearing all white.
Maybe it is too much to ask
That we only have one side.

SUMMER

You crashed into my winter heart
Like the hottest day of summer,
And the heatwave, it never stopped.
Who knew that my heart could withstand
Beating while engulfed in fire
Or that I could not be burned up
By the fever of desire.
But just like the weather, we changed,
And our autumn soon set in.
You were a season in my life,
And even seasons have to end.

3 A.M.

I woke up again
At three in the morning
And couldn't fall back asleep.
While tossing and turning
My mind began wandering,
Circling memories of you.

Of those late nights talking
And later nights exploring,
Back when being awake
At three in the morning
To spend some time with you
Was better than dreaming.

But another hour passes
I, no closer to dozing
As sleep evades my grasp
Because you're not here
To keep me company,
And never will be again.

RESTLESS

My soul yearns for a grander adventure,
But my mind wishes for a lazy day.
My weary heart yearns for precious moments
But my spirit can't take anymore.

Why can't the world fit in my backyard?
Why to live must I waste my life away?
Why does love always have to come with pain?
My spirit can't take it anymore.

CATCH ME

Why does love feel like
"Catch me if you can?"
Jumping through hoops
And dodging obstacles,
It's a mad, daring race,
Through hills and valleys
Over canyons and oceans,
And by the time you realize
You're the only one in the race
And there is no finish line,
You're already out of gas.

Nonsense

We can spend all day
And most of the night
Trying to make some sense of it all.

We can waste all year
And most of our lives
Trying to give meaning to it all.

Maybe it is just good sense
To simply love the nonsense.

Myths & Monsters

Humans tell stories
Of myths and monsters
And things that go bump in the night.
But these tales fail to warn us
And truly prepare us
For where the monsters truly hide.

For the real monsters
Are here by your side
Or just in your mind.

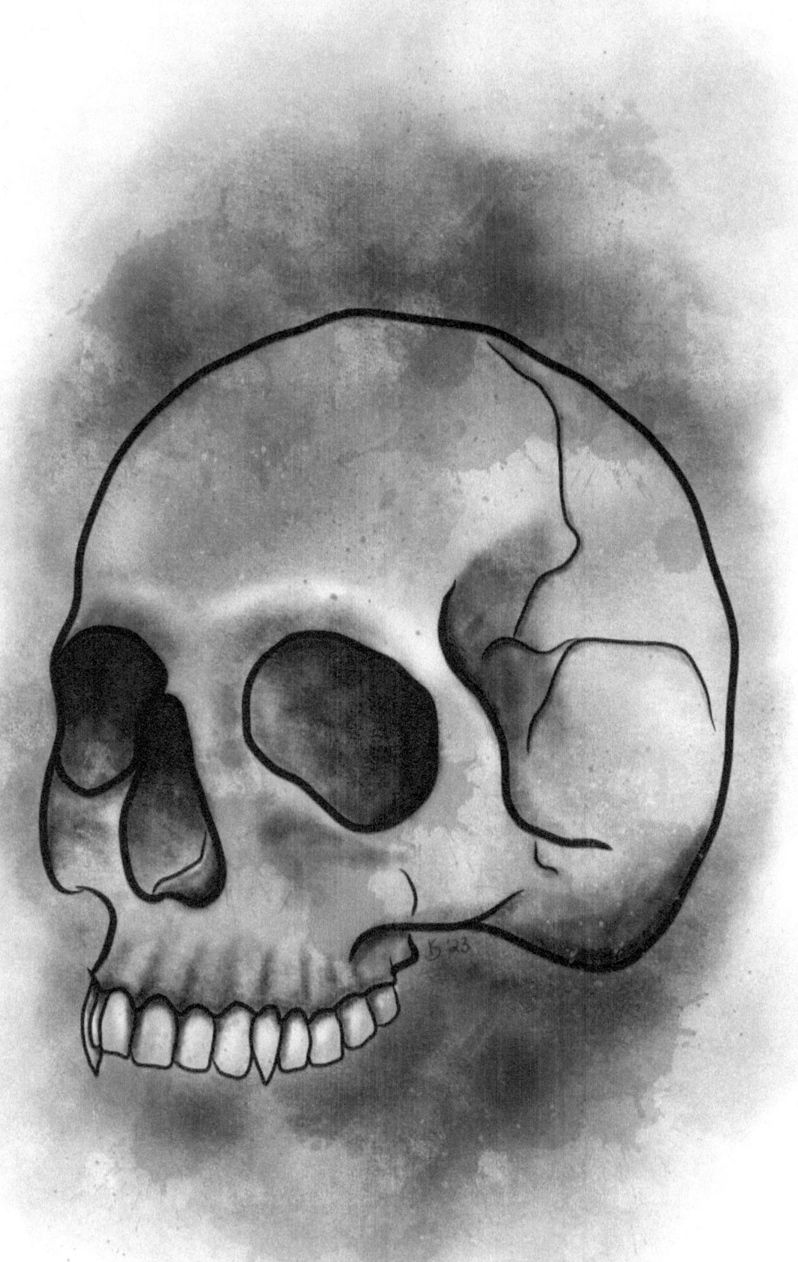

UNUS

Coarse sand flows like a river
Along crystal clear glass,
Swirling and tumbling down.
Each grain of sand a moment,
Gone in the blink of an eye,
But preserved forever in stone.
A lifetime, captured in a jar.

We Were Here

We were here.

We wrote our stories on paper
And etched our names in granite.
We painted our dreams on canvas
And carved our likeness in stone.

After we've long since departed,
When you see what we left behind,
May you feel it in what remains.
For if there was ever any doubt,

We were here.

Dreamer

Wake up, dreamer,
Get up, dreamer!
Wake up to the nightmare
That dreams don't come true.
Get up, dreamer,
Foolish dreamer!
The world is moving on
With or without you.

Like Hemingway

Another spray of blood
Across the keyboard
As my fingers dance,
Race, break, and bleed,
Trying to meet a deadline.

Sacrifices must be made
To breathe life into words:
A soul to begot more souls.

Such is the painful,
Beautiful life of an artist.

TOMORROW

There's always tomorrow,
I said,
Three years ago,
And tomorrow never came.

I still have the rest of my life,
I think,
As more time flies,
With nothing ever changing.

DISCORD

The discord of music
Meant to keep me focused
Whines and screeches
To unfamiliar notes
Matching the chaos
Of my scattered thoughts.

DENSE

To understand
Is a burden
Not carried by many,
For the weight of empathy
Can bring most men to their knees.

Being Human

Maybe I'm not cut out for this "human" thing,
    This 8 to 5,
    Daily grind,
    An hour drive,
    Killing the vibe,
    Slowly dying inside,
    Trying to survive
    Another day in paradise,
That we call life.

FOUND

Things that are lost can be found,
But more often than not remain
Out of reach of this mortal plane.

THOUGHT FULL

My mind is tumbling down the drink
With far too many thoughts to think.

The things that are, things that could be,
And things that are imagin'ry,

Memories from the distant past,
Knowing the present will not last,

All the catastrophes to come,
How fast it can all be undone.

I'm always feeling on the brink,
It makes it hard to get a wink,
(Perhaps I ought to see a shrink),
With far too many thoughts to think.

ONE VERSE

Would my poetry still rhyme
In the language of the trees
Or make sense if translated
Into the whispers of the wind.
Does the rain have a word for pain?
Would a flame know what I mean
When I try to describe forever?
What is the word for love in lunar?
If the universe could write poetry
Would it mean anything to me?

Borrowed

We are given borrowed lives
And live on borrowed time.
We form borrowed ties,
We speak borrowed lines.
And tell borrowed lies.

SCARS

We are not our scars,
Nor our bruises
Or our bite marks.
The sum of our parts
Are greater than
The tattered ribbons
Of our fragile hearts.

Bittersweet

Those quiet winds of change
Smell like rot and honey
To varying degrees
Depending on which way
Comes forth the telling breeze.

Away

I long for the day
When it's a dream I'm chasing—

Instead of running away
From the mistakes I'm making.

THE FAIRY RING

Believing in fairies
Is not so far fetched
If you've ever wandered far
And suddenly set your foot
Into the heart of the deep woods
Where all modern sounds fade away
And silence swallows the breaths you take
As though you came from *There*
And you are now in the
                         Here
Which is altogether different
Than where you were one step ago
It's like falling into a new dimension
Where dryads dance among the trees
And spirits flit among the leaves
And fairy folk ride the breeze—
If only your mortal eyes could see.

MY RAINBOW

I drape myself in black and white
And the occasional gray.
It's not monochrome,
But a dazzling display
Of all of the colors
From the night to the day.

EAGLE POINT

A

Rock perches on the edge of a cliff overlooking the river.
It possibly could have been there forever and a day.
Stepped on by native's footprints and scratched
At by the hungry paws of wild animals
Until I happened upon the scenic spot
And stood much taller than the rock.
From its resting place, you may see
The muddy, mighty Mississippi
Meandering between the lands
Called Illinois and Missouri
And through the solid dam
Where the churning water
Stirs up a buffet of fish
That terns and pelicans
And ducks and eagles
Dive and dip for a bite.
They look so small
From this height
And that is why
The place is
Referred to
As Eagle
Point.

Moor of Fear

LISTLESS

Listless, a feeling like
Sighs through tight lips
Sounding with a hiss
Of a slithering snake.
There's no escape
When a melancholy mind
Is made numb and mundane.

Weathered

Today, the rain fell,
But it was just wet.
We didn't need it,
Yet it still came;
No rhyme or reason
It rained all the same.

Today, the sun gave light,
But no enlightenment.
The shadows hid
No darker meaning.
Everything is as it is,
As if robbed of feeling.

UNBREAKABLE

When you've been shattered to pieces
All scattered across the floor,
And you think to yourself, this is the bottom;
You can't be broken down any more —

You'll learn the greatest truth of all:
There's no such thing as unbreakable.

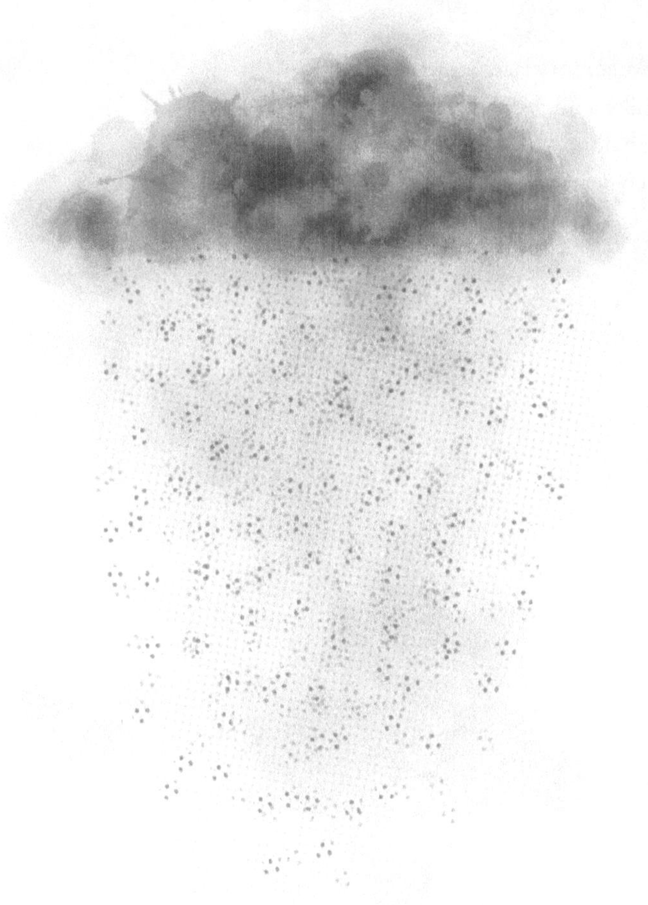

Before the Storm

I feel a change in the weather
Signaling a coming storm
In the way the wind rushes
From your strained lips
And the lightning flashes
In your narrowed eyes
The world holds its breath,
Preparing for the thunder.

KRAKEN

A memory rises from the deep
Like a mighty kraken once asleep
Shaking the world with rain and thunder
To drag my scattered mind asunder.

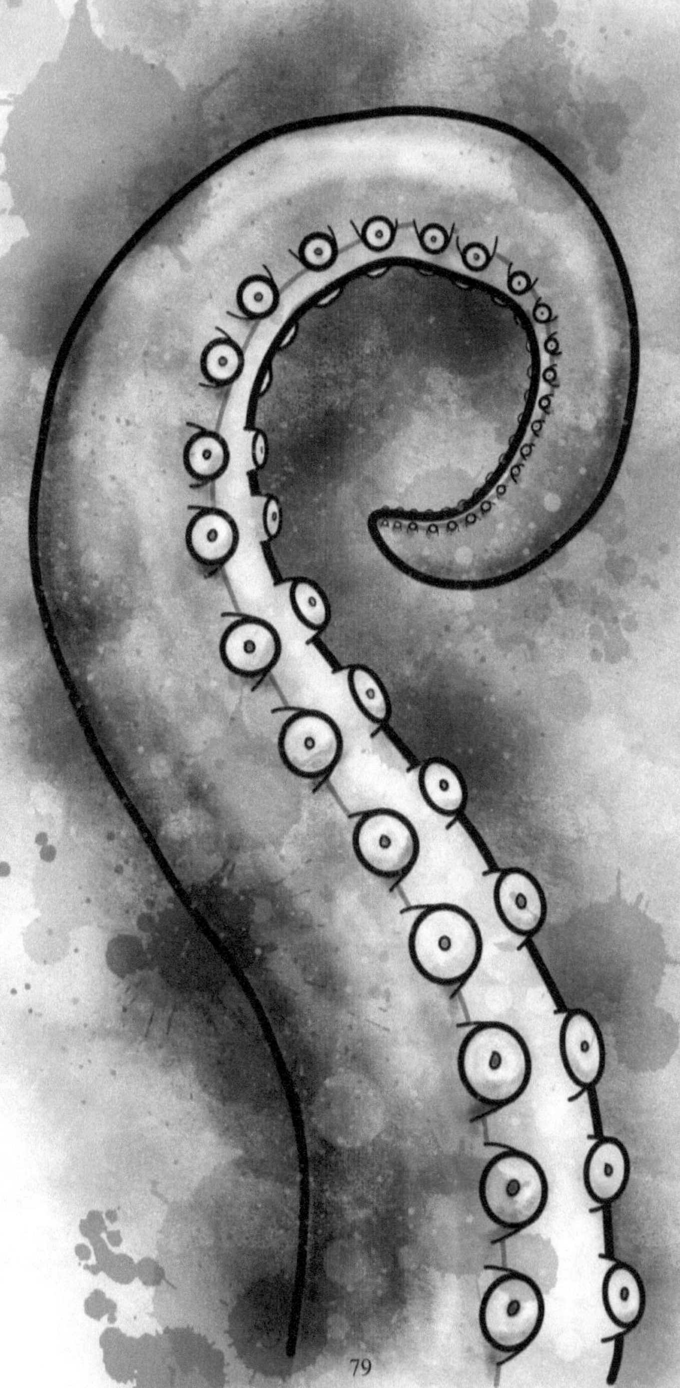

RETREAT

Strange,
I had been told
The best defense
And deadliest offense
Was a weapon called "kindness".

In battle, I feel ill-equipped
With such a fragile tool
Despite mastering the art
With all of my heart.

It seems my enemies
Are far more adept
With redirecting kindness
And turning it into malice
For their use against me.

Perhaps the greatest weapon of all
Is walking away before you fall.

BITE MY TONGUE

I bite my tongue for fear
That if I was to say
"I wish that you were here,"
You'd want to stay away.

Smiling Heart

If a heart can smile,
That means it has teeth.
If a heart has teeth,
That means it can bite.
If a heart can bite
Does that mean it eats?
If a heart devours,
Does it just eat meat?

Are we really sure,
It is not a beast?

Storm of Crows

I hope I'm not the only one
With an uncanny feeling inside
As if something is not quite right.
Tell me, can you hear it?

It sounds like a chorus of chalkboards screaming
In a storm cloud made of crows with onyx wings
Hailing fist-sized stones at stained glass windows.

I hope I'm not the only one.

BEFORE THE FALL

What hurts most of all isn't the fall,
But the memory of flying.

That innocent time in between,
Full of hope and opportunity
When the future is wide open
And just anything could happen.

When I fancied you thought me special,
When I thought you were letting me in,
When I saw in you what I wanted to see,
That is, you falling gently in love with me.

It isn't the fall that hurts at all,
But aching to live the dream again,
Before it all came crashing down.

PARALYSIS

Shadow in the doorway
With your wide, staring eyes,
Will you be my friend?

Shadow in the corner,
With your wide, toothy grin,
Are you just pretend?

Shadow in the closet
With your wide, reaching arms,
Is this how it ends?

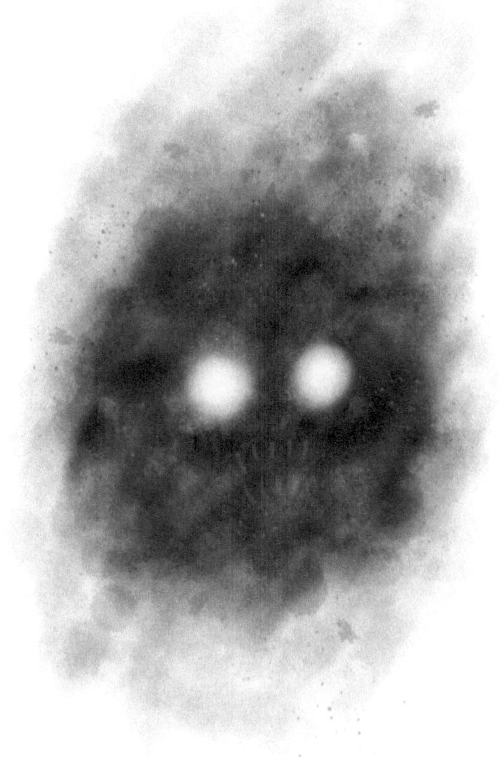

Immortality

I stand with Achilles,
Who led me to believe
The only immortality
We can hope to achieve
Is to persist as a memory
By living a great story.

SPIRALS

I'm spiraling again,
Twisting,
And knotting myself up.

I'm trapped again,
Stalling,
And frozen in fear.

I am tongue-tied,
Listless,
And lost in thoughts.

What if I'm not good enough?

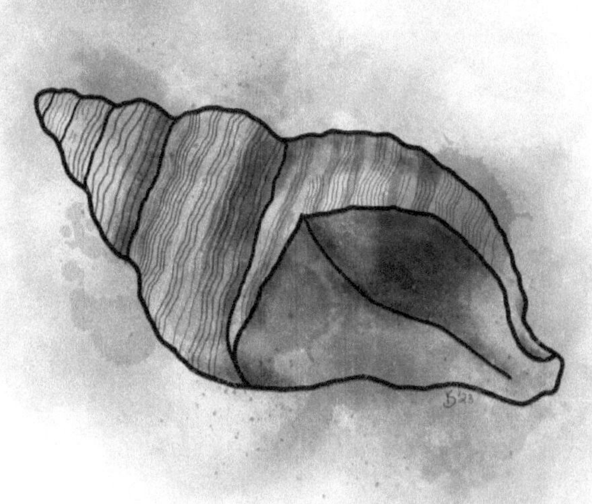

BE DRAGONS

Be sure you are prepared
For danger and adventure
Before wading into these waters

For we are off the beaten path,
Beyond the edge of the mental map
From this moment forth, beware:

Here there be dragons.

THE DAY THE SKY DIED

I opened my eyes
One autumn night
After falling asleep on the lawn.

I checked the time,
It was a quarter past nine
And there was no sign of the dawn.

Not a cloud in the sky
Nor a star's early light
And nary a trace of the moon.

To this day no one knows
Why the sun never rose
If it's lost it will be too soon.

GHOST

Stuck somewhere in between
Holding fast and flying free,
Gripping tight and moving on,
Midnight madness and breaking dawn.

SECOND FIDDLE

I'm just a little bittle
Getting caught in the middle
Of a big taradiddle.

Looking a little whittle
Like it might be a tittle
Bit more than I can fiddle.

As You Lay Dying

As you lay dying in a hospital bed,
I knew not where I could turn to,
For if you were to leave this world,
I would find myself all alone.

I was not ready to just let you go;
I was not ready to fly on my own.
There were still so many things to learn
And still more adventures to go on.

This could not be how it comes to an end
With you wasting away on a hospital bed.

I did not want to lie by praying
To a god I did not believe in,
But there was always someone who
Could fix any problem we faced,
The one I believed in most of all
And so I started praying to you:

The person I could always count on
To get us through the darkest times,
For if anyone could save our lives,
I only trusted you to pull us through.

I prayed to you with all my heart
As you lay dying in a hospital bed,
And dare I say, you heard me calling,
And you opened your eyes again.

SILENCE ECHOES

Silence is deafening
And speaks much more
Than words ever could.

Silence can mean anything.

That you are busy.
That you are not free.
That you don't need me.
That you do not see.

That I am not a priority.

Silence echoes in my mind
With all my insecurities;
Clattering and sputtering,
Whirling and crashing,

Until, finally, it is broken
By meaningless chatter
That says nothing.

Pool of Love

Shape of a Soul II.

My soul comprised of rain clouds
Knew sunny days for a time,
Whenever it came close to you.
Where I was gray and stormy,
You were glowing and bright,
Shining more powerful than the sun
That it was almost hard to look at.
And the most beautiful thing I ever seen.

My dark clouds were drawn to it
Like a moth to a flame
And when they got too close,
Your sunlight burned them away.
And for the first time, perhaps ever,
My soul knew a sunny day.
The rain, it paused, and the world breathed
Air dry and warm. It was blinding.
Perhaps, if you brought me fair weather,
And I sent rain to relieve your drought,
We would find ourselves in balance,
Two separate lives made together whole.

But you did not want to stop burning.
You wanted to burn hotter still,
Get lost in flames and banish night.
And I was far from a wildfire.

SECOND LOOK

I had only one question for you,
And one question only
That would tell me what I needed to know.
One question I could not voice,
Because I didn't think you'd understand
What I was actually trying to ask.

Do you see me?

Do you see me
For who I am
And what I've done
And how I feel,

Or do you see someone else,
Someone I remind you of,
Someone that hurt you
Or scared you,
Someone with a shadow so large
That I am dwarfed behind it,
Obscured in darkness,
So you cannot see me.

Are you blinded by them,
By the memory,
By the feeling.

Or do you see *me?*

Or have you seen me all along?

Then, perhaps, I was wrong.

∃ ❤ ⇐ ⇒
(OR, THERE EXISTS LOVE IF AND ONLY IF)

By my calculations,
It just made sense.
The numbers added up.
You plus me equaled
Laughter
Happiness
Peace.
The cause was observable,
The effect was measurable,
The results were repeatable.
Every time we came together
The bond was mutual.
The chemistry was reactive
Without being explosive,
Stable and refined.
If love could be defined,
In equations and numbers,
Then the results were clear.
True love was possible
Between you and I.
However,
There are two sides to every equation,
And I failed to take that into account.
There was one thing I forgot about,
One factor that made it all fall apart:
Your feelings had to equal mine.
The odds could only add up
If you wanted them to,
And without that essential component,
All answers came up as errors,
My proofs went up in smoke.
The numbers lost their value,
And the possibilities were null.
Perhaps love can't be rationalized after all.

So-Called Love

I am weary of this almost love,
This not-enough love,
This could-have-been love.
And if-only love.

I am tired of this one-sided love
This ill-timed love
This over-thinking love
And just-friends love.

I yearn for that first-sight love
That star-struck love
That once-in-a-lifetime love
And do-anything love.

I need a little bit of that true love
That cupid's-arrow love
That it-must-be-fate love
And only-you love.

None of that too-good-to-be-true love
Only give me that happily-ever-after love.

TELL ME

Tell me is there someone kinder
Who gives you their time and patience
Without asking for anything in return.

Tell me is there someone sweeter
Who smiles at every word you speak
Even when you have nothing to say.

Tell me is there someone fairer
With perfect hair and dolly eyes
That you cannot help but stare.

Tell me is there someone better
With love in their golden heart
To keep your soul warm at night.

Just give me a name,
Just one person only,
And I will find some peace
At last.

But if you can't,
Say my name.

Say my name.

FIRE IN THE HOLE

I say, be wary and be careful!
To gaze into this bottomless pit
You will surely lose yourself
As I have, many a time before.

Suppose you are a brave one,
To cast your eyes in the chasm.
Your reward, if you are lucky,
Is the greatest treasure of all,

For in that perilous void
Beyond the deepest darks,
There lies a heart on fire.
Yours to covet, if you dare.

HALF-BLIND

They say love is blind,
But that is only half true.
Love was born with two eyes.

Indeed, one of them is blind,
And sees not what is there.

The other sees things unseen;
Those things that never were.

In a single, fateful glance,
Love can both be blinded
By red flags and warning signs
While at the same time
Seeing signals of invitation,
Of affection, that do not exist.

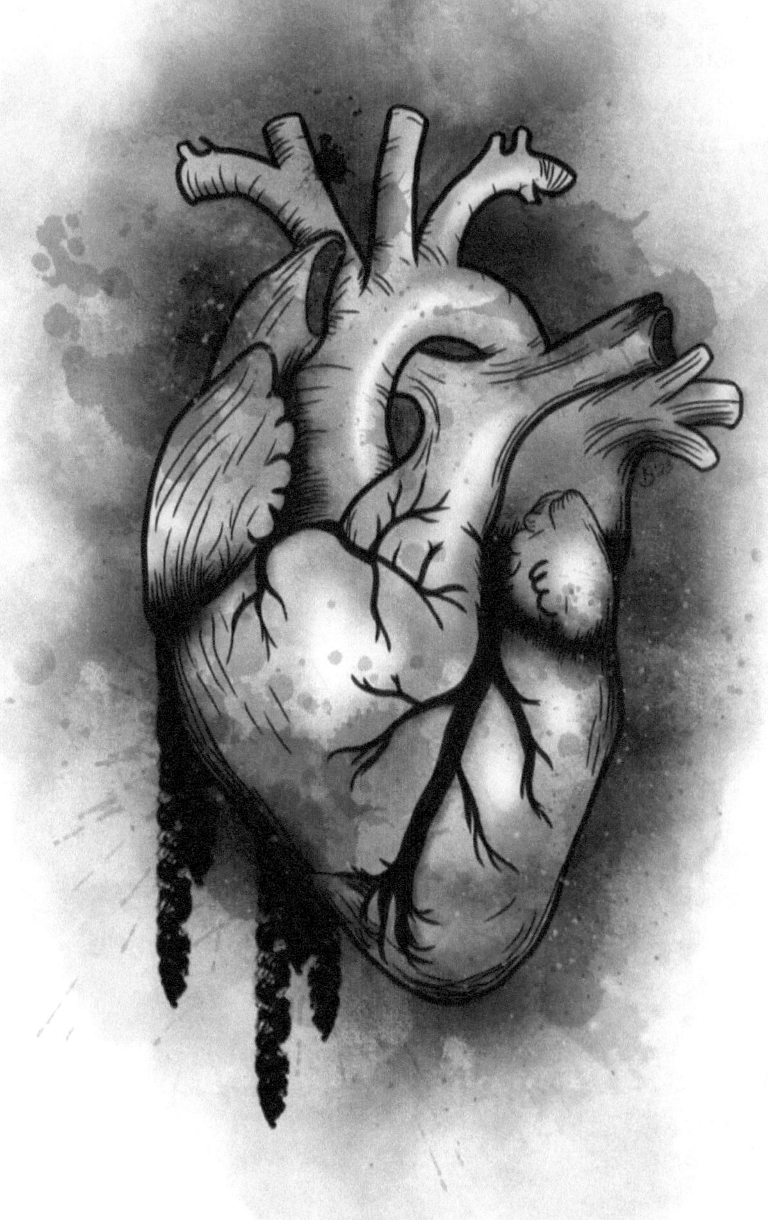

SMOKE STAINS

I will do my best to remember,
Remember you as you were.
Some days it will be hard,
And I hope you will forgive me
If I use your name in vain.
In turn, I will try and forgive you,
Even if now it is too late.

CUPID

I did it,
I confess.

I killed Cupid,
And I'd do it again.

He came at me with a bow
And silver-tipped arrow
Laced with that poison no. 9.

Really, it was self-defense.

THREE LITTLE WORDS

"I need you"
Is a paltry phrase
Of no real import,
For it robs us of the choice.

Needing you is like needing air,
Or water, or a bite to eat.
Things we need to live,
But not to make life worth living.

So instead say,
"I want you"
To tell me how you feel,
For then I'll know,
Without a doubt,
That you chose me,
Not because you had to,
But because this makes you happy.

DISTRACTION

When we both needed a distraction,
We found each other
And it was like we'd always been.
Not a day went by without speaking,
Every scar was shown and explored.
You knew me
And I knew you
Perhaps more than we understood.

When I needed someone to talk to,
You never failed to be there,
Because you, too, needed to fill a void,
A silence too big to carry alone.
But it was only a distraction.

In time, you had to deal with your demons,
The ones you had been putting off.
And me, I needed to focus
On the future I'd only been dreaming.
Just as quickly as we came together,
In a day, we drifted apart,
Pursuing our own ideas of happiness
Separate from one another.

I still wonder, some sleepless nights,
If we could have been more
Than just distractions,
But then it's time to get up
And leave you to my memory.

UNWORTHY

The longer that I wait for you
To realize I am worthy,
The more I start to realize
You are not worth my time.

The more I try to show you
That I am good enough
The more I start to question
If you're good enough for me.

I fear by the time you open your eyes,
My sights will no longer be on you.

CHEMISTRY

I wish that I could make you see
I'm not in love, but I'd love to be,
But that's not fair to you or me.
It all comes down to chemistry.

But if you were to ask of me
To be with you or to be free,
I know what my answer'd be:
I would be yours, entirely.

TIGHTROPE

There is a fine line
Between romance
And madness;
Obsession,
And affection.
We ride that line
Like a tightrope.

A Hundred Times

If words lose meaning
The more they are said
When I say "I love you"
For the hundredth time
Are you tired of it yet?

Autumn

Most people sigh
When summer dies,
But I breathe a sigh of relief
For when the leaves fall
And nights grow long
I find a reflection of me.

Afterword – The Year of the Deluge

*I*n the year of 1993, the mighty Mississippi River flooded its banks and spread out over 30,000 square miles. It was one of the greatest deluges in its history, second only to the great flood of 1927. By October of 1993, the flood waters finally started to recede—and that was the month and year that I was born.

My mother and father were fishing on the Mississippi River near Louisiana, Missouri during the height of the Flood of '93. Of course, this means that my mother was pregnant with me at that time. Before I was even born, I was being gently rocked by flood waters while my parents fished off their old jon boat. They camped along the flooded banks in a cramped camper for a week during that summer. Perhaps it is no wonder that I am drawn to the high, muddy water and the sound of the rain. The flood is in my blood.

The river is in my father's blood, too. His family took him to the Mississippi River at a young age and fell in love with the water and wildlife. In turn, he instilled that in me. Many a summer day was spent boating on the Mississippi until one day Dad decided he was tired of the 45-minute drive to get there. He started searching for a small house to buy— "a river shack," he said—so we could spend days out on the river without having to camp. Instead, he found a 2600-square-foot ranch-style home at an unbeatable price with an incredible view. It was the closest house to the river in that neighborhood. The nearest boat ramp is a two-minute drive away. An 11-acre wildlife conservation beach along the water stretches almost half a mile just behind the home. The location was perfect. That home became our River House. I was 12 years old at the time.

We owned that house during the 2008 flood, which nearly rivaled the Flood of '93. The river came up into our yard, about four feet away from our back porch, and twelve feet away from the house itself. You couldn't get much closer to the river than that. We were able to fish right out of our backyard. Where we lived, the 2008 flood lasted for weeks. At one point, we were worried enough to sandbag around the porch to prevent any damage to it (but it didn't get that far). In 2019, another flood rose just slightly higher than the 2008 flood, but it only lasted a few days.

The Mississippi doesn't get much closer than that!

When I started college, I moved into the River House full-time and have been living there ever since. Every day my eyes lay upon the flowing water. It is changing all of the time. For a moment it can be smooth like glass, and the next it is dark and turbulent. There are several places where the current regularly runs backward along eddies and islands. Floods are common. They don't get into the yard very often, but over the past decade there hasn't been a year where the river stayed inside its normal banks all summer. High water records seem meant to be broken. The deluges have become normal now.

W arm steam rises off the Mississippi River after a sudden cold snowfall.

Most cultures around the world tell a story of a huge storm that threatened to flood the whole world—The Deluge itself that Noah's Ark was supposedly built to escape. Even the oldest recorded written story that we have discovered, The Epic of Gilgamesh, has such a tale within it. A flood can damage the land, homes, and people when its banks run over. According to Britannica, the 1927 Mississippi River flood killed approximately 250 people and further displaced 750,000. However, it also inspired songs, like "The Levee Breaks" by Joe McCoy and Memphis Minnie (later covered by Led Zeppelin), as well as "Louisiana 1927" by Randy Newman. The rolling waters are both dangerous and inspiring, capable of both tremendous strength and calm beauty.

They also served as the inspiration for this poetry book. Like the mighty Mississippi, sometimes emotions can overwhelm us, drown us, and overflow out of us. Sometimes our levees break that we built up to contain them. Our emotions can whisk us away like a river, drag us down like a sea serpent, and spin us around like a whirlpool. However, there also is calm, peace, and growth to be had from the rain. Life flourishes where there is water. We cannot live without it.

When I first conceived the theme of this poetry collection, I called it "Drowning in the Deluge". Alliteration is my jam, and I'm fascinated by the archaic word "deluge". However, as time passed, I realized: just because you're in the midst of a flood, doesn't mean you have to be drowning. I simply changed the title to "In the Deluge". It's a subtle shift, but an important one. Whether we ended up here by choice or by force, we are here, in the flood. We might even be underwater, but we are not drowning. It is a lot of water, but we are weathering it. Maybe there are days where it feels like drowning, but maybe other days we're trying to dive deeper. Some days we are floating adrift. Sometimes we're at the bottom where it's so dark we can't see, and sometimes we're so close to the surface we can breach it. We are always in it, and maybe it's even in us.

Come hell or high water, we will weather it.

Acknowledgments

My dedication page for this collection rings quite true: every single person who has stirred my heart, mind, and soul deserves credit for this book. Good or bad, my interactions with people and the world shaped who I am today and what I choose to create.

However, there are some people and groups that deserve to be called out by name. These are the good ones. The folks that stuck around, built me up, and cheered me on. The folks that shared their wisdom, time, and kindness without asking for anything in return.

Ryan P. Freeman, who inadvertently provided me with the confidence and knowledge I needed to leap headlong into the writing community by his founding a little organization called The Hannibal Writers Guild. Without that first-ever guild meeting in January of 2018, I wouldn't be the writer I am today.

The St. Louis Writers Guild, whose members are the biggest bunch of positive, supportive, and knowledgeable people I've ever met. Their motto of "You have friends here" is no understatement; I found many friends there.

The Hannibal Writers Guild, whose members inspire me not just to keep writing, but to be a leader one can look up to and learn from.

The River Poets Society, f/k/a The Poetry Barn, whose members helped me become confident enough to call myself a poet.

J.R. Rogue, who wrote this collection's foreword. Her dedication to her craft despite all hardships and "floods" that try to interfere is something to aspire to. She was the perfect soul to introduce this collection.

My mother, who passed before she could see this collection, and who instilled in me a love of reading.

And my father, who would sooner use a book as fire-starter than to read it, and yet wholeheartedly supports me all the same.

About the Poet

*D*ana Lockhart grew up on the outskirts of a town of 199 people, but the small-town life couldn't contain her spirit. She yearned for something more adventurous and worthwhile, and, more than anything, for her voice to be heard.

After completing her degree, she went out into the world to try and make a name for herself, but she's still trying to find out where she belongs. She has since sought careers in helping others, including in local government, non-profits, and legal services. Her proudest achievement is being elected the first vice president of the Hannibal Writers Guild in 2018, and later the president in 2019. She writes with the intent to share ideas, inspiration, and meaning with her readers.

In the Deluge is her debut poetry collection and she has more in the works. Dana Lockhart primarily writes urban fantasy, ranging from young adult to adult. She's also been known to write a short story or poem now and then. She lives a modest life on the banks of the Mississippi River with her two cats, Nimble and Binx.

Appendix and Contents

Illustrations
(only full page illustrations are named)

Please consider rating and reviewing *In the Deluge*. Every review helps an author achieve their dreams!

Find out what project Dana is working on next on her website. Follow her on social media if you like books, games, and cute cats.

www.danalockhart.com
@DanaLockhart411
danalockhart411@gmail.com

www.ingramcontent.com/pod-product-compliance
Lightning Source LLC
Chambersburg PA
CBHW031146130726
47988CB00006B/2560